GRANDSON OF NORWEGIAN JOKES

by E.C. "Red" Stangland

published by

NORSE PRESS

Box 1554
Sioux Falls, S.D. 5
U.S.A.

D1711992

Illustrated by Don Steinpeck

Second printing
ISBN 0-9602692-7-4

For extra copies of GRANDSON OF NORWEGIAN JOKES, see your book dealer. If unable to locate, just send $2.25 per copy to:

NORSE PRESS
BOX 1554
SIOUX FALLS, SD 57101
PRICE INCLUDES POSTAGE

See page 48 in this book for a brief list of Scandinavian fun items available from Norse Press including T-Shirts, other joke books about Norskies, Swedes, Danes, Finns, etc.

FOREWORD

Once again we pay tribute to those wonderfully quaint folks known as NORWEGIANS. . . those hardy Vikings who have inspired an entirely unique brand of folk humor. Who else but Norwegians could provide the identity of the fabled Hagar the Horrible of cartoon fame? A Frenchman? A Yugoslav? No . . . Hagar just **had** to be Norwegian.

Now. . . getting to Norwegian Jokes, and this, our third joke book listing the silly things we say about Norwegians. First, we feel obliged to make it "perfectly clear" that our jokes are NOT intended in any way to ridicule Norway, Norwegians, or people of Norwegian descent. In fact, we consider the jokes a tribute to the Norwegian sense of humor and the stolid Norwegian character.

We have heard at least two explanations as to why Norwegians don't ordinarily take offense at these jokes. One theory says that Norwegians are very humble people and are quite accustomed to being baited, picked on, or otherwise twitted in some manner. The other theory we've heard is that Norwegians have such a strong ego that they can't possibly imagine anyone SERIOUSLY considering that any of these jokes could be literally true.

Well, take your pick on which conjecture might be correct. Or provide your own explanation.

As author and editor, I take very seriously the responsiblitity of maintaining the difference between humor and ridicule. So, I take the position that since thousands upon thousands of people of Norwegian descent have received or purchased our joke books, there is a certain amount of implied sanction of this particular form of humor. As we say, this is actually FOLK HUMOR in the vein of Mark Twain and other purveyors of tall tales and exaggeration. Paul Bunyan fables are examples of humor and exaggeration blended to make a folk tale.

So it is that we ask that you accept GRANDSON OF NORWEGIAN JOKES as an outgrowth of story telling by and about a proud people. . . the Norwegians.

E.C. "Red" Stangland, FBN
(Full blooded Norsky)

A DOG NAMED SEX
(Written by a Norwegian)

For protection, my father got me a German Shepherd dog. Ven he found out I vas Norwegian, da dog bit me. He vas a vonderful vatch dog. Vun night vhile I vas being held up by a robber, da dog vatched.

Most people who have dogs call dem Rover or Spot. I called my dog "Sex." As I later found out, Sex is an embarrassing name. Vun day I took Sex for a valk and he ran away from me. I spent hours looking for da dog. A cop came over and asked me, "What are you doing in the alley at 4 in the morning?" I replied, "Looking for Sex." My case comes up Thursday.

Vun day I vent to City Hall to get a dog license, and told the clerk, "I vould like a license for Sex." He said, "I would like one too." So, I said, "But dis is a dog." And he said, "I don't care how she looks." So I said, "You don't understand; I've had Sex since I vas two years old." He said, "You must have been a very strong baby."

I told him dat vhen my vife and I separated, ve vent to court to fight for custody of da dog. I said, "Your Honor, I had Sex before I vas married." And he said, "Me too."

Den I told him dat after I got married, Sex left me; he said, "Me too." Vhen I told him dat vun time I had Sex on TV, he said, "Show off!" I told him it vas a contest. He said, "You should have sold tickets."

I also told da judge about da time vhen my vife and I vere on our honeymoon and ve took along da dog. I told da clerk dat I vanted a room to sleep in and anodder room for Sex. Da clerk said dat every room in da motel vas for Sex.

Den, I said, "You don't understand. Sex keeps me avake at night." And da clerk said, "Me too."

I give up!

Tina applied for a job in an office. In hiring her, the boss explained, "In six months, you will be eligible for a raise, provided you work diligently."
Tina muttered under her breath, "I knew dere was a catch to it."

Ole's son Hjalmar didn't graduate from the top half of his class...but he had the distinction of being in the half that made the TOP half possible.

Some one asked Lars if he knew who the greatest inventors were.
"Sure," said Lars, "Dere vas dat Irish guy, Pat Pending; and da Russian guy, U.S. Regpatoff."

Sven: Olson got a bicycle for his wife.
Tryg: How in da vorld did he get such a lucky trade?

Philosophy of Ole: "Money don't buy happiness...but needer does poverty."

4

Ole and Lena had nine very handsome children. Then came a tenth child...but this one...to be blunt...was extremely ugly. Ole thought about it for some time, then one day, he confronted Lena. "Lena...tell me da truth...is dat last youngster really mine?"

"Yah, Ole," confessed Lena. "Dat last baby is yours. But da others AREN'T."

Ole: Tell me, Doctor. How do I stand?
Doctor: That's what puzzles me, Ole.

Ole and Lars were talking politics. Said Ole: "Yah, dat Pressident Reagan...he's doing da vork of five men. Da tree Stooges...and Abbott and Costello."

They were planning to put up a statute of Uncle Torvald over in Norway. But they ran out of Silly Putty.

Ole: Torvald, what do you tink about LSD?
Torvald: Vell, he vas a pretty decent President.
Ole: No...I mean da dope.
Torvald: Oh, him. Vell, dey kicked him out of office, so I suppose ve're all done vid him.
Ole: What do you tink about da farm bill?
Torvald: Vell, if ve owe it, I s'pose ve should pay it.

5

Ole reports he recently had a nightmare...his wife and Dolly Parton were fighting over him. And his wife won.

Uncle Torvald was lecturing little Lars on his bad manners.
"Lars...you are eating like a little pig. You know what a little pig is, don't you?"
"Yah," said little Lars. "A little pig is a hog's little boy."

A Norwegian had to bail out of an airplane. He pulled the first ripcord, but nothing happened. So he pulled the emergency ripcord...and again, nothing happened. Bewildered, he looked around as he rapidly approached the ground. To his amazement, he saw another man...ascending upward at a rapid rate. "Hey..." yelled the Norwegian..."what do you know about parachutes?" "Not much," called back the other man..."I happened to specialize in gas stoves."

Ole says that Lena is on a banana diet. "She hasn't lost any weight," reports Ole..."but you should see her climb trees."

Ole: What do you get when you mix holy water and prune juice?
Knute: Vell, I tink you get a religious movement.

Arnie: Say Torvald, I understand you and your wife celebrated your 25th anniversary last month. I suppose you had a party...killed a chicken or something?

Torvald: No...ve vouldn't do dat. I don't believe in making a chicken suffer for something dat happened 25 years ago.

Professor: In our experiment, we put a worm in water, and another worm in a glass of whiskey. Now...you see, the worm in the water is healthy, active and swimming around. On the other hand, the worm in the whiskey is already dead. Now, what does that prove to you?

Ole: Vell, it proves dat if you drink viskey...you won't have vorms.

The doctor told Lars he had six months to live. Lars said he couldn't pay the bill. So the Doctor gave him another six months.

SPEAKER: In this day and age, it is hazardous to use any jokes about ethnic groups. Many politicians and other public figures have gotten into trouble by using ethnic jokes. It is much safer to tell a story using a lost civilization like the Hittites. You've read about the Hittites in the Bible. They no longer exist. So, with your permission, I would like to tell you a story about two Hittites named Ole and Lars.

Lars: I heard that you had to shoot your dog, Fido.
Was he mad?
Ole: Vell, he vasnt exactly pleased about it.

Ole: What did you get your wife for her birthday,
Torvald?
Torvald: A box of chocolates.
Ole: Was she surprised?
Torvald: I'll say so...she vas expecting a mink coat.

Torvald says that nowadays when he feels romantic he goes to bed with TWO women. "Dat vay," he
explains, "if I fall asleep, dey can talk to each odder."

Wisdom of Ole: "Money isn't everything...Henry
Ford, vid all dat money...billions of dollars...never
owned a Cadillac."

Lars: What do you think about AWACS?
Torvald: Vell, at our house, ve use Yohnson's vax.

This is a sign hung in Ole's Cafe in Decorah:
Please don't criticize da coffee.
  You may be old and veak someday yourself.

Did you hear about the Norwegian who thought
that Manual Labor was the President of Mexico?

A Norwegian flasher announced he was planning
to retire. But his friends talked him into sticking it
out for another year.

As you may know, Norway is the new Oil Kingdom
with off-shore drilling bringing millions if not
billions to the country. A publication sent to us
from Norway tells of how the Swedes have been
telling jokes about Norwegians on the oil plat-
forms throwing breadcrumbs at the helicopters.
But the Norwegians had a comeback, telling how
the Swedish helicopter pilots swoop down to pick
up the bread crumbs.

A Norwegian airlines pilot complained that the
runway in Minneapolis was only 100 feet long. "I
can't see why dey made it so short...ven dey made
it tree miles vide."

Have you seen the Norwegian Toronado?
It's a '54 Chevy with snow tires on the front.

Ole and Lars worked on a construction crew. One day Lars noticed that the foreman always left the project about an hour early. "Say Ole," suggested Lars. "Why don't WE take off a little early too...yust like da foreman." So they agreed to try it. As soon as Ole got home, he looked all over for Lena. Finally he opened the bedroom door...and there she was in bed with the foreman. Ole silently closed the door and tiptoed out of the house. The next day he confronted Lars. "Ve better not try anudder stunt like ve did yesterday. I almost got caught."

An ocean liner hit an ice berg at sea and rapidly sank. Among the survivors were a Norwegian, an Englishman and a Frenchman in a life raft. As they drifted, the Norwegian idly put his hand in the water. All of a sudden, he grasped a bottle floating in the sea. So he pulled out the cork...and out came a genie. "I've been in that bottle for ten thousand years," said the Genie. "As a reward, I'll give each of you ONE wish."

"That's easy," said the Frenchman. "I wish to be back in Paris."

POOF...he was gone.

"And I," said the Englishman, "wish to be back in London."

POOF...the Englishman was gone.

"Vell," said the Norwegian, after pondering a bit. "It's kinda lonesome out here...so I vish dose odder two guys ver back here to help me decide."

Ole: Say Torvald...you're hair is getting kinda thin on top. Don't you think you maybe ought get a toupee?

Torvald: Heck no...I don't see no sense in getting a new top for a convertible...when da motor's shot.

A Pole kidnapped a Norwegian kid...so he sent him home with a ransom note. The kid's parents sent him back with the money.

Torvald: How do you recognize Ronald McDonald in a nudist camp?

Lars: By da sesame seeds on his buns.

Lena was a servant girl for the Johnson family. One night she was preparing to serve dinner...and bumped into Mr. Johnson in the doorway to the dining room. Going back to the kitchen, she ran into Sonny Johnson. Both Sonny Johnson and Mr. Johnson chided her a bit for being in the way. Sensitive Lena took it to heart and went to Mrs. Johnson. Sobbing, she said, "Mrs. Yohnson...I'm going to leave here...I'm in da family's way."

Misunderstanding, Mrs. Johnson exclaimed, "Why Lena...when did it happen...?"

"Oh," said Lena..."it was vunce in da dining room vid Mr. Yohnson and vunce in the kitchen vid Sonny."

An oil drilling company in Texas had a big well fire. Even Red Adair couldn't put it out. They offered a reward of $50,000. A Norwegian fire department from Southern Texas offered to come up to try to put out the fire. As they came roaring up the highway, they turned off into the oil field...not only UP to the oil fire, but right IN it. The Norwegian firemen jumped out of their fire truck and began thrashing the fire with their jackets. Miraculously, the fire was put out by these Norwegians! As the superintendent reacted with amazement, he led Ole, the fire chief, into the company office where he made out a check for $50,000. "Congratulations, Ole," he said. "Here's your $50,000. Now, what do you plan to do with the money?" "Vell," said Ole, "first of all ve vill haff to get da brakes fixed on our fire truck."

Success Story: Ole says, "When I came to dis country, I didn't have a nickel. Now...I have a nickel."

A Norwegian kid was delivering the newspaper to his new customer.
"What's your name, son?" inquired the customer.
"Lyndon Johnson," said the kid.
"Well, that's a pretty well known name, isn't it?" remarked the customer.
"It oughta be," said the Norwegian youngster. "I've been delivering papers on dis route for over six months."

Ole and Lena had been married 12 years with no off-spring. One day Lena announced that Ole was going to become a papa. Uff Da! Ole vas so over-joyed...in fact, he exclaimed that he was going down to the paper to put in a notice so their friends would know the good news. When he got back home, Lena asked, "Did you put da notice in da paper, Ole?" "Yah I did," said Ole. "How much did it cost?" asked Lena. "$900," answered Ole. "Uff da!" exclaimed Lena. "Dat's an awful lot. Vot did day tell you?" "Vell," said Ole, "Da lady asked me 'how many insertions?' So, I said three times a week for twelve years."

Lars went to the doctor for a checkup. The doctor pronounced him fit as a fiddle for a man of 75 years. "How old was your father when he died?" inquired the doctor.

"Who says he's dead?" answered Lars. "He's 95 and in terrific shape. Rides a bike and golfs every day."

"Remarkable," commented the doctor. "How old was HIS father when he died?"

"Who says he's dead?" said Lars. "He's 120 years old and really in fantastic shape. Swims every day and goes bowling. In fact, he's getting married next week."

"Why in the world would a man of 120 years of age WANT to get married?" asked the doctor.

"He doesn't WANT to," answered Lars. "He HAS to."

Elofson, the undertaker, was hauling a corpse to the cemetery in Duluth, Minnesota. As the hearse was slowly progressing up the steep hill, the rear door accidentally came open and the casket, which was on rollers, went careening down the hill...with Elofson in hot pursuit. Just as the casket was heading into the door of a drugstore, Elofson ran breathlessly up to the druggist, gasping, "Say, Doc...have you got anything that will stop this coffin?"

Lena: Vhy do you go on da balcony vhen I sing? Don't you like to hear me sing?

Ole   Vell, I yust vant da neighbors to see I'm not beating my vife.

Helga went down town to buy a single shoe to send to her son, Johan, who was in the army. (He'd written home that he'd grown another foot.)

Ole and Lena took little Lars to church for the first time. After the services, they asked him how he liked it. "Vell," said little Lars, "Da music progarm was OK, but da commercial vas too long."

Knute: I vould like to marry you. Vill you have me, Kari?

Kari: Vell, leave your name and address and if notting better shows up, I vill notify you.

A Norwegian found a bottle on the street, rubbed it a bit to dust it off...suddenly a genie popped out, thanked the Norwegian, and told him he had three wishes. For his first wish...the Norwegian asked for a brand new red convertible, with all kinds of chrome and a terrific stereo and many other gadgets. Poof...instantly he was in a beautiful red convertible so gorgeous you wouldn't believe it. Then he said, "I wish I had a beautiful red haired gal in this car with me to help me enjoy it. Poof...instantly an absolutely ravishing, gorgeous young gal, right beside him. Then, he tuned in a station on his car radio. Beautiful music. As the song ended, a commercial came on. In his joy, the Norwegian began singing along with the commercial, "I wish I was an Oscar Mayer weiner....."

Lars and Tena invited a well-to-do Uncle for dinner. Little Arnie looked him over and finally approached the old Uncle with a request. "Uncle Knute...vill you make a noise like a frog for me?" said Arnie. "Vy in da vorld do you vant me to make a noise like a frog?" exclaimed the Uncle. "Because," said Arnie, "Papa says ve are going to get a lot of money ven you croak!"

ODE TO DA NORVEGIANS
by Julie Stangeland

Vel, da Svedes, dey got a lot of ham
Vich means a lot of hogs,
And da Danes, dey got a million of
Dose great big whopping dogs

And da Finns, dey got da reindeer
And dey got da sheep and cows,
But da Norskies had dose Wiking ships
Vit dragons on da prows.

Dey used dem to go pilla-ying;
Dey'd land and den say, "Hi!
Say, vere's da gold and silver?
Hand it over now, or fry!"

Dose Wikings plundered everyvun!
Dey really had a kick!
Dey vere the first guys to know how
To really get rich qvick.

And ven dey got to England,
Dis is vat dey did:
Dey left behind deir nouns and werbs
And lots of liddle kids.

Dey conquered everybody in
Da vorld, and den, to boot,
Dey even got dese real svell names
Like Olaf, Sven and Knute.

But, cuz da U.S. people like
Dose old guys vit dark hair
Ven Norskies run for president
Dey yust don't have a prayer.

So dat's my Norskie poem
And it makes me feel so sad
Dat everyvun can't be Norvegian
Yust like my dear old Dad.

(Julie is an English teacher at Long Beach, Calif.
University. She is the daughter of a shirt-tail cousin, Jim
Stangeland)

NORWEGIAN SNO-MOBILE

SPECIAL DELUX MODEL
ONLY
$49.50 Plus Tax

Little Ole once had a cross-eyed school teacher.
She had a terrible time keeping her pupils straight.

Svenson was an incurable optimist. No matter what horrible event people would tell him about, Svenson would invariably say, "Vell, it could have been worse." One day two of his cronies told Svenson about the terrible tragedy where Bjarne Olsson was killed by Olaf Hegermoe after Bjarne had been fooling around with Hegermoe's wife. "Vell," said Svenson in his usual manner, "It could have been vorse." "Vorse? How could it have been vorse?" asked the crony. "Vell," said Svenson, "If it had been da night before, it vould have been ME."

Bakkedahl was musing on the park bench. "Vunce I had everything...a nice apartment..the love of a tender young voman. And den my vife had to valk in and spoil it."

Ole say: "Dere vas a time ven a fool and his money were soon parted. Nowadays it happens to everyvun."

Lena says: "Vimmen spend ⅓ of their life looking for a husband...den they spend another ⅔ vundering vhere he is."

A young Norwegian bride brought a dish for approval of her new husband. Said she, "Da two tings I prepare best are meatballs and peach pie.."
Norwegian: Hmmmm. And vhich vun is dis?

Uncle Torvald made a killing in the market recently...he shot his broker.

Torvald asked the local banker, "Vots da latest dope on Wall Street?"
Answered the banker, sourly, "My son in law."

Torvald says that Americans are funny: "First day put sugar in a glass to.make it sveet; den, a twist of lemon to make it sour, gin to make it varm dem up, and ice to cool it off. Den dey say, "Here's to you," and drink it demselves."

Hjalmar, the fighter, was doing badly in the ring, having taken several nasty blows. He was finally put on the canvas by a right to the jaw. While the referee counted, Hjalmar's manager whispered, "Don't get up til eight." Hjalmar raised himself weakly and mumbled, "Vat time is it NOW?"

Torvald comments: "A mortgage is a gimmick dat speeds up da months and slows down da years."

Also from Torvald: "Scientists say dat man evolved from da monkey over several million years...but a voman can make a monkey out of a man in a couple seconds."

Torvald says: Bad news travels fast...unless you mail it.

Sven: Have you heard...dat dey elected a Pole to be Pope?
Ole: Yah, it's about time...dose Catlicks have had it long enough.

Undertaker: What can we do for you?
Norwegian: I vant to make arrangements for my funeral to be buried at sea.
Undertaker: Why do you want to be buried at sea?
Norwegian: To get back at my vife. She said dat vhen I died, she was going to dance on my grave!"

At the meeting of the Loyal Order of Norwegian Sons of Eric, the Secretary got up before the lodge to announce: "Tonight ve vill not be honored vid da presence of our most illustrious and powerful, all-seeing and omnipotent Grand Ruler of da Lodge. His vife von't let him out tonight."

A Norwegian was consulted to help a Japanese firm name their new compact car. The Norwegian asked how soon they would require the name; he was advised it was needed within two weeks.
"Dot soon?" he asked.
   The Japanese misunderstood and thought that was the name he had chosen...so they put their own spelling on the car...the Datsun.

A Norwegian appeared before the judge to have his name changed.
"What is your name now?" asked the Judge.
"Ole Stinks," replied the Norwegian.
"Hmmm...I can see why you want it changed. What do you want it changed to."
"Lars."

How do Norwegians count?
"Vun, Two, Tree, Four, anudder, anudder, anudder, anudder."

Lars and Kari got divorced for religious reasons. She worshipped money...and he didn't have any.

A carnival had come to town and the strong man was challenging the villagers in this Norwegian community. "I will squeeze this lemon," declared the strong man, "and if anyone can squeeze ONE drop more from it after I am done...will be given one thouand dollars."

Several people tried it...but to no avail. Finally, a little, shriveled up guy stepped forward and said he'd like to try. The strong man squeezed a lemon with all his might, reducing it almost to pulp. Then he handed the remains to the little weak-looking man...who then squeezed and squeezed and squeezed...finally extracting ONE drop of lemon juice. The strong man was amazed, and while handing him the thousand dollars revealed that this was the first time he had had to forfeit the money. "Tell me, sir," said the strong man, "what do you do for a living?" Said the little guy, in a quavering voice, "I'm the treasurer at the Norwegian Lutheran church."

A knock on the door. Ole goes to answer it. He encounters a masked man with a gun.
"Are you a robber?" inquires Ole.
"No...I'm a rapist."
Ole: "Lena...it's for you."

Torleiv was a cannon polisher at the court house for 20 years. Finally, when he had saved some money, he quit his job. Next thing that the people in the town heard...Torleiv had bought his own cannon. "Always wanted to go into business for myself," was his explanation.

Mikkelson was a traveling salsman and one day his car got stalled on a country road. A nearby farm house proved to be some Norwegians who invited him to stay the night. For supper, the menu included rommegrot. Although Mikkelson was crazy about rommegrot, he restrained himself and took only two helpings. At bedtime, the farmer explained they only had one bed, so Mikkelson would have to sleep between the farmer and his wife. About 3 in the morning, the farmer had to get up to tend to some farrowing sows. The farmer's wife tapped Mikkelson on the shoulder and whispered, "Now's your chance." So, Mikkelson tiptoed downstairs to the refrigerator and finished off the rommegrot!

Karl: Do you wake up grouchy?
  Ole: No...I let her sleep.

Little Rasmus was late for school. The teacher asked him to explain.
"Vell, I had to take our registered bull over to da neighbors," said Rasmus.
"Why couldn't your father do it?" inquired the teacher.
Answered Rasmus, "'Cause Pa ain't registered."

THE SAGA OF U.T. (UNCLE TORVALD)

You've hear about "E.T." now, read about the story of Uncle Torvald, abandoned by an escaping Norwegian fishing schooner carrying contraband lutefisk.

Here Red Stangland advises Uncle Torvald to attempt to return to his native land, Norway. Torvald is broke, so Red offers to hitch-hike with him.

Here we see Uncle Torvald tying his shoe the Norwegian way as he and Red prepare for their journey.

U.T. (Torvald) is shown crossing the bridge on the River Kwai. He explains to Red: "Babies along the River Kwai are called Kwai Babies."

Here we see U.T. (Torvald) contacting Norway by a radio transmitter disguised as an umbrella. The line is busy.

U.T. (Torvald) & Red are seen traveling through jungle grass in darkest Africa. Torvald wants to capture a zebra for a pet and name him "Spot".

Arriving home U.T. (Torvald) is greeted by his dog, Carpenter, so named "Because he does odd jobs around the house."

U.T. (Torvald) is happy at last in his simple home in Norway. (At one time, Torvald was Norway's most famous organ player. Then his monkey died.)

END

Ole Torkelson is quite a clown...always joking. Even in the hospital. When he was laid up in the hospital and someone knocked at the door, he'd call out, "Who goes dere...friend or enema?"

Wise sayings from Ole: "Any guy can have a wife...but only the Ice Man has his pick."

Doctor: You seem to be healthy for a man of 75. How is your love life?
Knute: Vell, almost every day.
Doctor: That's remarkable. Tell me more.
Knute: Vell, almost on Monday, almost on Tuesday, almost on Vednesday, and so on.

Ole and Lena made a good pair. He was knock kneed and she was bow legged. When they walked together, they spelled "OX".

Ole says he wears dark glasses around the house because it bothers him to see his wife work so hard.

More of same: "It's not the HIGH cost of living that gets us in trouble...it's the cost of HIGH LIVING."

Magnus was inspecting little Hjalmar's report card. It was pretty grim. Finally, Magnus saw a bright note: "Vell, Hjalmar...vun ting in your favor...vid a report card like dis, it's a cinch you're not cheating."

Sven: Teacher, I don't tink I deserved a zero on dis test.
Teacher: Neither do I...but it's the lowest grade I can give you.

Lars: Vaitress...bring me some vatery scrambled eggs, den burn some toast, den bring me some veak coffee.
Waitress: Yes sir, right away.
Lars: Don't be too fast...and vhile you're at it...nag me awhile...I'm homesick for my vife.

Knute: Caddy...how would you haff played dat last shot?
Caddy: Under an assumed name.

Dagmar was trying to lose weight, so she took up horseback riding. After the first week, the horse lost 10 pounds.

Momma Johnson: Eat your spinach, Hjalmar. It'll put color in your cheeks.
Hjalmar: Who vants green cheeks.

Lena is some cook. It takes her an hour to cook minute rice.
(She once tried to open an egg with a can opener).

Ole and Lars were shipwrecked on a small island in the Pacific. Also stranded was an Irishman named Kelly. As time went on, the men grew accustomed to being marooned and led a good life on the island. Finally, the Irishman died. The two Norwegians were puzzled about how to give Kelly a proper funeral since he had been a Catholic. Ole volunteered to do the service if Lars would dig the grave. Ole said he had once listened to a Catholic church service, so after Lars dug a big hole, Ole put on his best ministerial tone: "In da name of da Father, the son, and (shoving Kelly's body with a foot) IN DA HOLE HE GOES!"

Lars say, "No vun can say I'm a quitter...I stay on the job 'til I get fired."

Ole says, "I never get mad vhen I play golf...if I miss a shot, I yust laugh. Yesterday I laughed 115 times."

Ole and Lena went to have a family picture taken. The photographer told Lena to look natural...so she posed with her hand in Ole's pocket.

You've heard about bad cooks...Lena actually keeps Alka Seltzer on **tap.**

Brita: I heard dat Ole proposed to you and dat you accepted. Did he tell you dat he had proposed to ME first?

Lena: Vell, no; but he did mention dat he had done a lot of foolish tings before ve met.

Lars says, "I married my vife because of a mental problem. I vas out of my mind at da time."

Ole and Lena were going home from the grocery store with Ole pushing the baby carriage. Suddenly Lena exclaimed..."Ole...we've got da wrong baby!" "SSHHH" said Ole..."dis is a better buggy."

Lars says: "Gunderson must have a kidney condition...everytime dey bring da check in a restaruant, he has to go to da men's room.

Ralph: Arnie, what's the difference between ignorance and apathy?
Arnie: I don't know...and I don't care!

Folks around town say that Ole has the Midas touch; everything he touches turns into a muffler.

Nels was talking to a neighbor, Roskeland, and mentioned that a Swedish neighbor, Blomquist, was sending his son to "Gus Davis College." Roskeland was puzzled because he'd never heard of such a school. So one day he asked Blomquist what school he was sending his son to. Replied Blomquist, "It's up dere in St. Peter...Gustavus Adolphus."

Lena went into a drug store and asked for Talcum Powder.
Asked the druggist, "Mennens?"
"No, silly," said Lena..."Vimmens."

Hans called Ole long distance and asked him to loan him $5.
"I can't hear you, Hans," said Ole. "Dis line must be bad."
The operator broke in to say, "I can hear him perfectly clear."
"Vell," said Ole, "If you can hear him so good, vhy don't YOU lend him da five dollars."

Hear about the Norwegian who disappearerd?
He had just put on a pair of Odor Eaters.

Rasmussen, who had a stuttering problem, was expounding on the problems of the world. "I-I-I-I tink-k-k dat ve S-s-s-h-o-u-ld Qv-v-v-v-it sending money all-I-I-I- over da v-v-v-v-orld and Y-y-y-y-ust keep our money t-t-t-t-t-o home."
"Oh sure," snorted Kasperson..."Dat's easy for YOU to say."

Lena: Ve don't know vhat to do vit Ole...he tinks he's a chicken.
Tena: Vell den, you maybe should take him to a psychiatrist. He needs help.
Lena: I know...but ve need da eggs.

Helga: Vhat is a "Wooden Wedding?"
Knute: "I'm not sure...I tink dat is vhen two Poles get married."

A Norwegian had the misfortune while on a drinking spree...to drink a quart of varnish. He died, of course. But he had a beautiful finish.

The teacher was writing some sentences on the blackboard when she a dropped her chalk. As she bent over to pick it up, little Arnie piped up, "Teacher...I can see two inches above your knee." Outraged, the teacher said, "Arnie, for your impertinence, you are expelled from school for one week." Shortly, the teacher dropped the chalk again and bent over to pick it up. This time, little Ralph spoke up, "Teacher...I can see FOUR inches above your knee." Infuriated once again, the teacher ordered little Ralph to be expelled for TWO weeks. Ten minutes later the teacher once again dropped the chalk; and again, stooped over to pick it up. As she raised up, she noticed little Halvor grabbing his school books and heading toward the door. "Halvor, where are you going?" asked the teacher. Answered Halvor..."I'm going home, teacher, my school days are over."

Ole has a digital alarm...Lena pokes him with a finger to wake him.

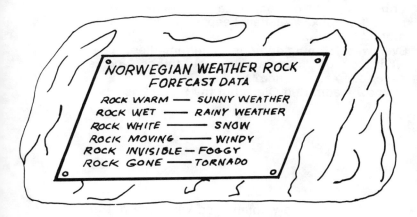

Make your own Norwegian Weather Rock

Why depend on unreliable TV forecasts?
Have your own never-fail method of determing the weather.

Just find a suitable rock and put a label on it with the information pictured above.

A Norwegian was bragging up America to his cronies in a bar in Norway. "Yah, it is vundferful in America. You go into a bar, have a few free drinks...den you go in da back room and have free sex. Den you do go back and have some more free drinks...den you go back in da back room and have more free sex. You can keep it up like dat all night."

Sven was listening dubiously and remarked, "Ole, what do you know about dese things...you've never been to America?"

"I know," admitted Ole..."but my Sister has."

This Norwegian lived way, way out in the woods in Minnesota...seldom came into town. Finally when the snow went out, the Norwegian and his wife went to Duluth. They spent nearly two hours watching a microwave oven. Finally, the Norwegian got up in disgust. "Come on, Ma," he said, "If dis is vat television is like, dey can have it."

Knute called the Salvation Army: "Do you save bad girls there?"

"Yes we do," came the answer.

"Vell," said Knute..."save me vun for Saturday night."

Ole calls his dog CARPENTER. Because he does odd jobs around the house.

A Swedish woman sent her husband downtown to buy a Lazy Boy rocker. He came back with a Norwegian guitar player.

A Norwegian was dickering on a new Cadillac. The salesman told him it would cost $16,000, but if he could decide that day, he would be allowed 10% off. The Norwegian, not being willing to admit he couldn't figure such high mathematics, told the salesman he'd have to think it over for a few minutes. So he walked across the street to a cafe. He sat sipping on coffee, trying to figure it out with a pencil and paper. Finally, about to give up, he called the waitress over to see if she could help him. "Say, Vaitress," said the Norwegian, "How much vould you take off for 10 percent of $16,000?" The waitress grinned and asked demurely, "Would my earrings get in the way?"

How do you get 20 Norwegians into a Volkswagen?
--You throw a quarter into the back seat.

Ole was commenting on the way the world is today, "It's REELY sumting...da vay da young things go around with fancy hair-dos and skin tight pants. And da vimmen are even vorse."

Ole once had an implement dealership in Wisconsin. His motto was: "Ve stand behind all of our implements...vid de exception of da manure spreader."

A Norwegian discovered he had mice in the house, so he set a trap. Being a bit thrifty, he used as bait...a picture of a piece of cheese. When he checked the trap next morning he found...a picture of a mouse!

A Norwegian was recently arrested for passing bogus $2 bills. The way he did it was to erase the zero from $20 bills.

Ole says: "Be very careful ven a guy tells you he is boss at home. Some day he might lie to you about sumting important."

Sven was flying on an airliner when the plane encountered extremely turbulent conditions. A nervous old lady, expecting disaster, turned around to Sven and implored, "Please do something religious." So, Sven started a Bingo game.

"Weesie" Ness of Virginia Beach, VA., submitted this little gem:

Back in the pioneer days there was a Norwegian settler named Ole. He built his family a nice cabin, and then commenced to till the soil. For his family's safety, Ole installed a large bell, instructing his wife to ring it if an extreme emergency arose. The next week, Ole heard the bell ringing, so he grabbed his rifle and ran madly to the house. There was Lena, fetching one of the youngsters out of the well. Ole was furious because he didn't consider it a dire emergency. A few days later, Ole was again summoned by the ringing bell. When he got to the house, Ole breathlessly asked what the trouble was. "Oh, da cows got into da corn," explained Lena. Again, Ole was furious, chastising his wife for calling him home on such a flimsy "emergency." About a week later, Ole again heard the clanging bell. But this time he took his time, finishing up a row he'd been plowing. As he leisurely strolled home, he stopped briefly to pick some blueberries. Then, as he came over a hill, he saw his home in flames. All the livestock had been slaughtered, and his wife and children wounded. As he gazed on the scene, Ole was heard to comment: "Velll...DAT'S more like it!"

A Norwegian calls up his Doctor and says, "Every morning at 5 I have a B.M."
"Fine," said the Doctor. "That's very healthy. What seems to be your problem?"
"Vell," said the Norwegian. "I don't vake up 'till six."

Ole: Call da manager...I can't eat dis food.
Waitress: It's no use...he won't eat it either.

Dagfinn loved crossword puzzles. When he died, his last request was to be buried 6 down and 3 across.

Ole: (Talking about Lena) Yah, she's yust like an angel. Alvays up in da air and harping about sum-ting.

Knute started a new business...it was the first time for him. As he sat admiring his shiny desk, he noticed someone coming in; so he busily picked up the phone and acted like he was taking a big order. After finishing the "call" he put down the phone and turned to the visitor: "Yes...what can I do for you?"
"I'm here to install the phone," answered the man.

The judge had just awarded a divorce to Lena who had charged non-support. He said to Ole, "I have decided to give your wife $400 a month for support." "Vell, dat's fine, Judge," said Ole. "And vunce in a while I'll try to chip in a few bucks myself."

Ingrid: Vould you like to see da ring dat Lars gave me?
Helga: It looks like a nice ring. And it must be a comfort to know dat he isn't a spend-thrift.

Helga: I bought dis dress for a ridiculous figure.
Kari: Vell, YOU said it...not me.

Also from Ole: "Vimmen get married so dey can make a homing pigeon out of a night Owl."

Lars was released from his employment so he asked for a letter of recommendation. The boss wrote: "Lars worked for us for five years. He is no longer working for us. We are very satisfied."

Uncle Torvald explains what happens when you cross a gorilla with a computer: "You get a Hairy Reasoner."

Torvald might be considered a little simple...he thinks that Assets are little donkies.

Ole says: "Never tell people your troubles. Half of dem don't care...and da odder half is glad it happened to you."

Kari: Ole, you remind me of da ocean.
Ole: You mean...vild, restless and romantic?
Kari: No...you make me sick!

Jens is on a new diet. He never eats while his wife is talking.

Sven lives in such a small town that the 7-11 is called "3½-5½".

Norwegians are always starting up businesses that are just a bit "different". For example, Uncle Torvald had some experiences in business that were not very successful. First, he opened a Tall Men's Shop in Tokyo. It folded. Then he manufactured a soft drink called "6 Up". After that, a produce called "Preparation G." (Other companies later changed the names and cleaned up.)
Two of Torvald's enterprises that almost made it: A car called the "Hard Bargain". (For people who like to drive a hard bargain.)
And then an insurance company called "Honesty Insurance." (Torvald advertised: "HONESTY IS THE BEST POLICY.")

Here are a couple of Norwegian jokes exported (or was it "**de**ported"?) from Norway.

Rolf Liland, who hails from Hop, Norway, asks: "How can you identify the pessimist Norwegian at the air field?" He's the one without a ripcord on his parachute because he figures it won't open anyway.

And the Norwegian optimist jumps without a parachute because he figures he can borrow one on the way down.

Ole was sent to prison for one year because he was caught taking some hogs that belonged to a neighbor. The day he left the farm to go to prison was a sad one. As he bravely bid goodbye to Lena, he said, "Lena, I'm leaving you and da hired man in charge of da farm til I get back."

Upon his release, Ole happily came back to the farm where he found things in good condition and the farm thriving. Even Lena seemed in fairly good spirits as she greeted him after his 12 months away. Lena served Ole some of his favorite lutefisk and lefse. As Ole gazed around the kitchen, he spotted a jar in the cupboard with 9 dollars and five soybeans in it.

"Lena," he queried, "Vhat is dat yar vid five soybeans in it?" "Oh, Ole," said Lena, "I have a confession to make. Vhen you vas in prison, I got awfly lonesome vidout you. So vhen I couldn't stand it so good, da hired man and me, vell, ve kinda got togetdder a few times. And vhen ve did, ve put a soybean in da yar."

Ole thought a minute, and told himself that in a year's time, five occasions weren't so bad that he couldn't forgive Lena. "But Lena," said Ole, "Vhat is da nine dollars for?"

"Vell, you see, vun day da market on soybeans vas up to nine dollars, so I yust sold off a bushel."

Hilda: Vhen ve vere younger, Lars, you used to nibble on my ear.
(Lars starts to leave the room)
Hilda: Vhere are you going, Lars?
Lars: Into da bedroom to get my teeth.

News item from OSLO: "The police here have arrested a Norwegian for selling 'Eternal Youth' pills. Records at the Oslo police station showed he was a repeat offender. He has been similarly charged in 1452, 1799, and 1935."

A Norwegian got on a TV quiz program. Said the Quizmaster, "and now for $20,000...can you tell me...HOW MANY D'S in "Here Comes the Bride?" The Norwegian scratched his head, shifted his weight from one foot to the other, gazed at the ceiling, and finally declared, "68."

"68?" exclaimed the Quizmaster. That is incorrect. But how did you arrive at 68?

The Norwegian answered by humming, "De De de de...De de de de....."

Ole offered Sven a pinch of Snoose.
"I don't chew da stuff," said Sven.
"What?" said Ole. "You used to chew snoose, usen't you?"

Lena was in the bathtub when the door bell rang.
"Who iss it?' she called out.
"Blind man," came the answer from the front door.
Lena got out of the tub, walked straight to the front door without so much as a stitch of clothes, and threw open the door.
There stood a man who asked, "Where do you want me to put these blinds, lady?"

Johan: You say it mentions tennis in da Bible. Vhere does it say dat?
Halvor: I forget where it is exactly...but it does mention dat Joseph served in Pharaoh's court.

Katrina was in her car, stopped at a traffic light. The light turned red, green, amber, and then red again. A cop standing on the corner was heard to comment, "Lady, let me know when you see a color you like."

Rasmus figures he better go on a diet. He was wearing a red, white and blue outfit...when someone came up and tried to put a letter in his mouth.

Mari: You look like a million dollars.
Karl: How's dat?
Mari: Green and wrinkled.

Knute claims that the first actor in history was Samson: "He brought down da house," comments Knute.

Did you hear about the Norwegian who couldn't spell very well?
--He spent all night in a WAREHOUSE.

Two Norwegians hi-jacked a submarine...then demanded $100,000 and two parachutes.

A Norwegian in our town took a bus trip from Wisconsin to California. He had to rest up for a couple of days due to "bus-lag."

A Norwegian girl went into a drug store and asked for talcum powder.
"Yes maam...walk this way," said the druggist, walking briskly down the aisle.
"Uff Da," said the girl. "If I could valk **dat** vay, I vouldn't need da talcum powder."

Ole was a businessman, and one day got a request from the government to fill out a form about his employees. One question asked: "How many employees do you have broken down by sex?"
When Ole filled out the answer, he wrote; "Practically all of dem."

Capt. Ragnar Folven from Sandnes tells about two Norwegians sitting in a park, one reading a newspaper. The other asks, "What date is it today?" To which the other responds, "I don't know." "But," says the first Norwegian, "can't you look in your paper?" "It's no use," says the other. "This is yesterday's paper."

Ole was out of work and in looking for a job, applied at the Dingaling Brothers Circus. The circus manager looked Ole over from head to toe, and then disclosed that they might be able to use Ole in the Human Cannonball act. "I think you'd work out fine, Ole," said the manager. "We could use a man of your caliber."

What do you call a Norwegian education?
----"Trivial Pursuit."

A nurse in the hospital came out to the waiting room to tell the Norwegian that his wife had just had a baby. "I'm happy to tell you that you have a little girl," said the nurse, "but I'm sorry that I have to tell you that one leg is a bit shorter than the other."
"Vell, dat's all right," responded the Norwegian. "Ve vere planning to call her 'Eileen' anyvay."

Here are three wise Old Norwegian sayings:
1. Never eat at a place called "Mom's"
2. Never play cards with a guy named "Doc."
3. Never buy fresh fish from a truck with Oklahoma license plates.

A Norwegian in our town was apprehended for stealing a lady's underskirt from the clothes line. The judge let him off, however, because "It was his first slip."

Ole and Lena attended a Gay Nineties party. Half of the people were gay...and rest were past 90.

An itinerant lawyer named Blaine Nels Simons was working on a case in a rural community. When his car broke down, he was forced to borrow a horse from a country preacher, Rev. Donald Anderson. The preacher gave Simons instructions on how to make the horse go and stop. "First, you say, 'Praise the Lord', and the horse will go. And to make him stop, just say, 'Amen'." So the lawyer started on his journey by saying, "Praise the Lord." And sure enough, the horse took off. In fact, on a fast gallop. This startled the lawyer to such an extent that when he began panicking because of the horse's speed, he forgot the word to make him stop. Just as the horse was careening toward a cliff, and appeared about to go over the cliff, the lawyer suddenly remembered the word, "Amen." And sure enough, the horse stopped right at the cliff's edge. With a huge sigh of relief, the lawyer mopped his brow and fervently uttered, "PRAISE THE LORD!"

ORDER BY MAIL
These fun novelties for
Norwegians & other Scandinavians

NORWEGIAN CROSSING
SIGNS 12'' x 12''
METAL $7.00
CARDBOARD $3.50

SEND FOR
FREE BROCHURE
ON CURRENT
PRICES OF
OUR NORWEGIAN
AND SWEDISH
T-SHIRTS,
BUMPER STICKERS,
ETC.

JOKE BOOKS
NORWEGIAN JOKES	$2.25
SON OF NORWEGIAN JOKES	$2.25
GRANDSON OF NORWEGIAN JOKES	$2.25
UFF DA JOKES	$2.25
MORE UFF DA JOKES	$2.25
POLISH JOKES	$2.25

ALL POST PAID

NORSE PRESS
BOX 1554, SIOUX FALLS, SD 57101